How to create your own animal sticker fun!

- On each page you will find stickers of fruit, flowers, feathers, fur, fungus, scales, spines, wings, waves, eggplants, eyeballs and much, much more!

- Choose your favorites to create your own portraits, fantasy animals and monsters, or fill in the silhouettes with designs and colors that fit your personal style!

- Use the stencils and patterns to create your own, unique stickers.

- You'll find plenty of space to design and re-use, re-stick, and re-create your decorative masterpieces. Forest creatures, sea monsters, farm animals, fruit fairies: It's all up to you!

How to use stencils to make your own stickers!

Begin by carefully removing the stencil page from the book.

1. Choose which stencil you would like to work with.

2. Pick a background pattern that suits your stencil.

3. Hold the stencil steady on top of your pattern, and trace completely around the edge with a pencil.

4. Carefully cut your shape out with scissors.

5. Remove your sticker from its backing.

6. Find the perfect spot and place your sticker!

7. Add other accessories and sticker eyes, or bring your sticker to life with markers, crayons, and pencils.

8. Step back and admire your work!

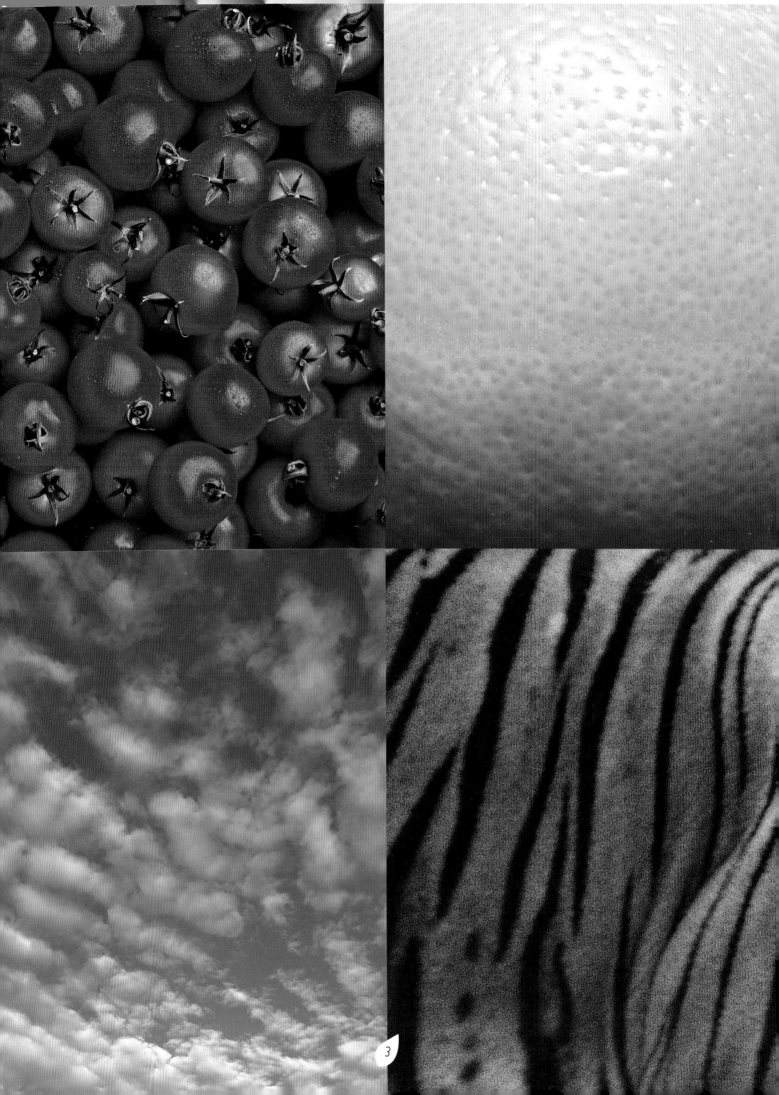

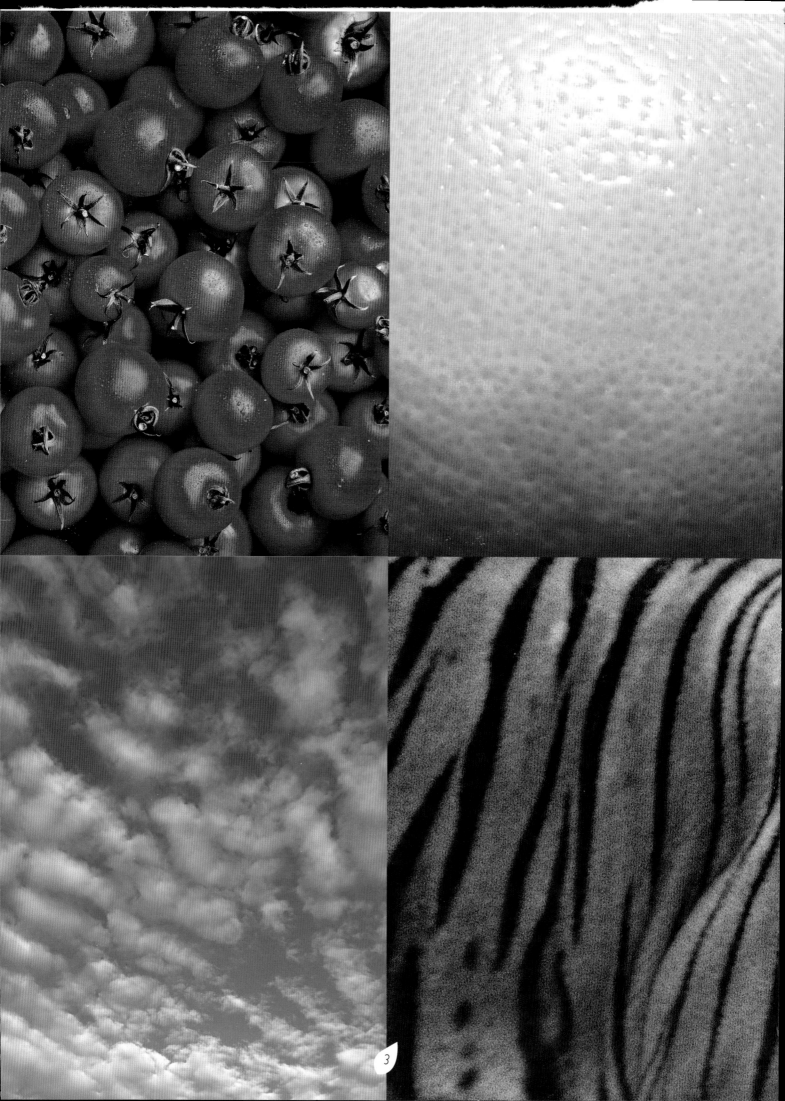

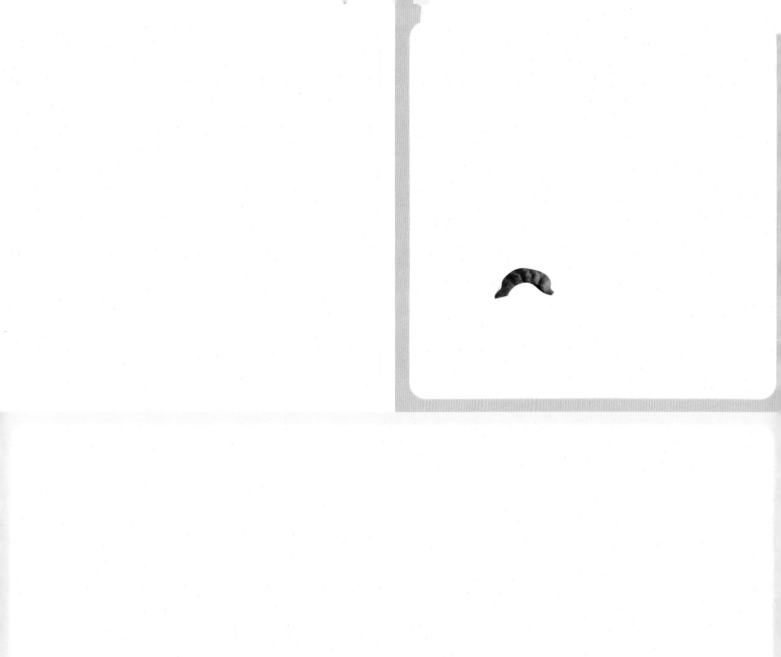

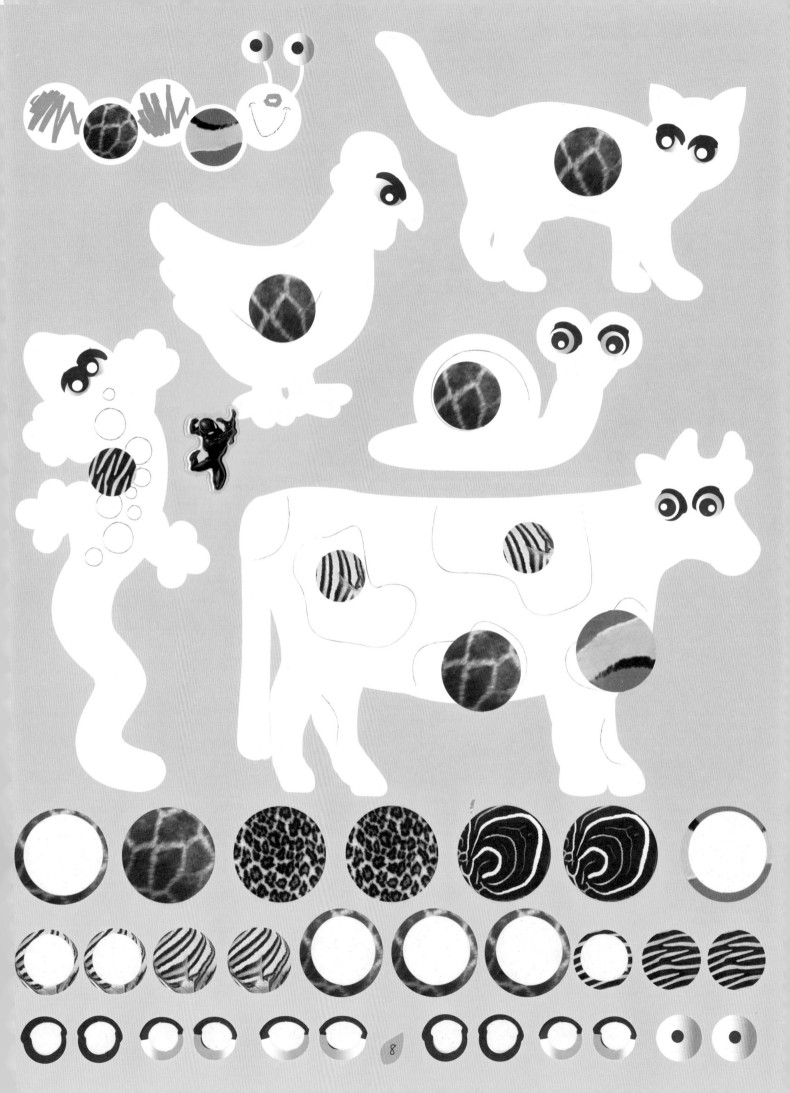

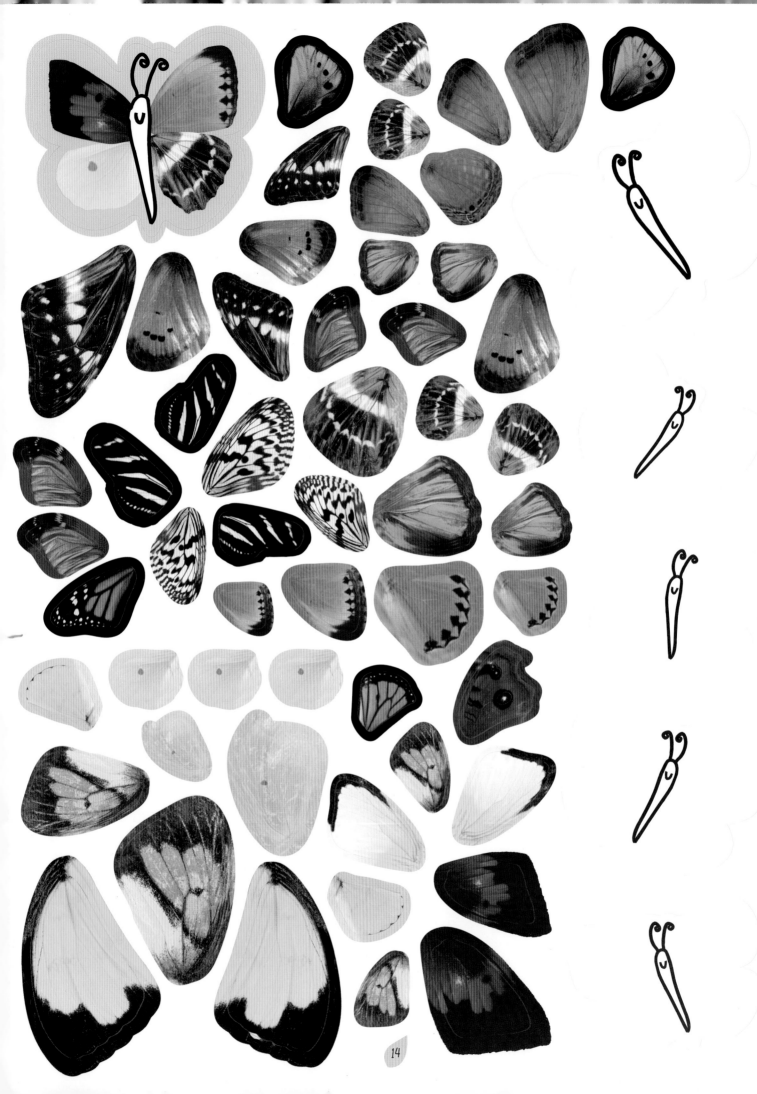

Create your own beautiful butterflies !